Also by Barbara Rose, PhD

Individual Power

If God Was like Man

Stop Being the String Along: A Relationship Guide to Being THE ONE

Know Yourself

If God Hears Me, I Want an Answer!

The Ultimate Guide To Self Love

Being an Awesome Parent Raising Awesome Teens

Get Over Him FAST

Being Enough NOW

Wisdom on the Other Side of Knowledge

Realigning Religion

Transforming the Unknown

I'm Not in this Life to Please You!

Your Loved Ones Hear You: Explanations about Life on the Other Side

The Rush to Spend

I Don't Need Your Permission to Live My Life!

Divine Intervention: The Cards Drawn from Your Soul

The Official Complete Guide to Higher Self Communication

BARBARA
ROSE, Ph.D.

The

Messiah's

Handbook

THE ROSE GROUP
Uplifting Humanity One Book at a Time ™

Barbara Rose, PhD

The Messiah's Handbook

The Rose Group
Uplifting Humanity One Book at a Time™
Florida, United States

ISBN-10: 0979516102
ISBN-13: 978-0-9795161-0-8

You may contact the author through her Web site:
www.borntoinspire.com

Health, Mind & Body > Self-Help > General
Health, Mind & Body > Self-Help > Self Esteem
Health, Mind & Body > Self-Help > Personal Transformation
Health, Mind & Body > Self-Help > Abuse
Health, Mind & Body > Self-Help > Motivationa

Interior and cover layout by Toni Williams
www.livinginbloom.com

CONTENTS

PREFACE

There was something indescribably holy about the evening of Passover in 2008. I was alone and felt deeply drawn to God in a manner different from the inner connection I usually felt during such an event. I felt a calling from deep in my soul that only communion with the divine, loving energy of God could edify.

As I sat down, words from God flowed into my mind . . . The Messiah's Handbook . . . I wondered for a moment if it might be my imagination providing the words. Wanting to be certain, I did a writing and asked God whether it was my imagination or, indeed, the name of another book given to me by

Him. The answer became crystal clear: I was being asked to bring through The Messiah's Handbook . . . for you.

As you read this book, pay attention to the feelings in the middle of your chest, the area of your heart, that which is linked to your higher self, soul. If you sense a loving, drawing feeling - as if you feel love and feel deeply drawn to feel even more - answers await you within these pages.

I am by no means anyone's leader. I align my will with divine will and bring through, for you, the words of God.

CHAPTER 1

WHY WOULD A MESSIAH NEED A HANDBOOK?

The day has dawned that humanity awakens from within. The feelings of aloneness cease, replaced by the peaceful flow of love. Why would a Messiah need a handbook? Your question is a wonderful one. The answer is to know which guidelines to follow, because certainly the Messiah was born a babe just like you.

The Messiah is among you, clothed in human attire, often wearing his heart on his sleeve (or her heart on her sleeve) . . . the emotions every human being feels are deeply felt by the Messiah, too.

There is a yearning to understand God, to understand the role God is to play during this lifetime. How is this lifetime vastly different from your previous lives?

The Soul's Growth

As a human being in the twenty-first century, you have lived many lifetimes prior to this one.

Many times, a far-away place beckons you, reigniting a sense of familiarity . . . as if, perhaps, you had been there before.

The opportunity is at hand for you to truly know who the Messiah is, the most important traits you will be able to recognize and the guidelines to follow within the role of the Messiah.

It will help you to refer to this handbook. It will help you when you ponder and wonder how sacred a role you play. It will remind you of the truth that you were aware of millennia ago: God is within you.

CHAPTER 2

❧

ADMISSION

As you acknowledge the spiritual calling of your soul, you sense that you are here for a far greater reason than even you may surmise at this time.

The blessed and the cursed are shown equal favor from you. The garments of society's status are transparent to you. Whether a person sits as head of state or alone in a shelter, each human being is seen by you through the eyes of equality.

The Realization

The first stage of acknowledging that each human being is as divine as the other is not a revelation; it is the realization of truth. How the eyes see with the heart - the compassion and care shown to everyone equally - is your first clue about being a Messiah.

The Laundry

What does laundry have to do with the Messiah?

The Messiah does not descend from the sky wearing an ever-clean robe. He wears clothes typical of the culture he was born into, as you do. She went to school because she had to, as you did. He played in the mud because he wanted to, as you might have done. So she had to put her muddied clothes in the laundry - as her mother asked - so they could be laundered, like yours are.

How Is the Messiah Different?

How, exactly, is the Messiah different from others?

Interestingly, the differences show that the Messiah has more qualities in common with the regular person than those that are different. We know that the Messiah has basic needs (like clothes and laundry) and feelings (he or she has cried, felt alone and rejected, hungry and thirsty, distressed and sad, as well as content and joyful).

And through it all, while enduring life's trials, circumstances, and lessons, the Messiah has come to know that the key difference is her or his ability to sustain the manifested spirit of love and compassion that all human beings, in one way or another, are endeavoring to experience as well.

The power of the Messiah is rooted in love, integrity, and care for all and exudes the deep desire to serve. When you feel a calling in your heart to make even the slightest difference, this is what the Messiah feels all of the time.

Differences and Similarities

Would it surprise you to know that you are not different from the Messiah? You are now realizing that your role in this lifetime carries blessings and responsibilities to yourself, as well as to others.

These traits found in the Messiah can also be found in you:

- A desire to know your purpose.

- A concern for those less fortunate.

- A desire to extend love to others who feel un-lovable.

- A caring heart that seeks to do good deeds be-cause you have placed yourself in the shoes of the person you are looking at and your heart knows the right thing to do.

- A sense of modesty and awareness that there is no reason to brag or boast. The making of a dif-ference - the rippling effect of even the tiniest dif-ference - brings joy into your heart, just like the Messiah's.

- A desire to evolve. You desire to know how to fulfill your greatest potential in accordance with divine will.

- A trust in the loving guidance you receive from God. Whether it is presented as a dream or the small voice within you that suddenly guides you from out of the blue, you are aware that you are being guided. And although it may not log-ically make sense at the time (such as the inner guidance to travel a different road home today than the one you usually travel), you know to follow that guidance.

You are given guidance the moment you need it, and you eagerly follow it because you know this guidance will keep you on the path that you desire most to follow. The inner guidance will keep you safe in the outer world.

The wisdom to understand the lesson of regret. You, just like me and exactly like the Messiah, have felt the regret of not following divine guidance - the ever-present, divine energy of God that manifests as the small voice within, a higher knowing, or higher consciousness.

CHAPTER 3

DEFINITIVE TRAITS

J ust what, exactly, are the definitive traits of the Messiah? And is there any way to discover who he or she is?

The definitive traits of the Messiah are courage, love, compassion, inwardly balanced conviction, divine certainty, and a desire to do what is appropriate for the highest good of all.

Divine love provides a depthless reservoir of care and compassion for all experiencing the difficulties of life on earth.

The Messiah receives and gives divine guidance to all people, even if they aren't willing to listen.

Never boastful, the Messiah allows each person to honor her or his truth.

The Messiah will never evangelize or insist that someone follow a specific religion or doctrine. The Messiah knows, as you do, that God exists equally in everyone, regardless of religion or doctrine. The divine in some is simply more obvious than in others and naturally fluctuates with changing conditions.

The desire to do only what is in accordance with love - divine will - brings you and the Messiah a step deeper into the ethereal knowing that nothing can be extinguished.

You know that you are here to serve. You care that your service makes a difference. You acknowledge that it is the divine working through you, rather than smugly taking credit and giving none in return to the divine source, that from which your guidance emanates.

The Messiah, like you, enjoys the feeling of childlike wonder, curiosity, and a playful and trusting demeanor.

When in contact with another person - or any other living creature - the Messiah, and you equally, do only what you know in your heart to be what you would want done to you.

The foods you eat are not governed by any time period or particular culture recorded in the Bible. The foods you eat are mostly "living, organic foods" - foods that replenish and nourish your body. You delight in feeding yourself well.

You pray for all life, and as you take your first bite of food, you have already asked in heartfelt prayer that every person throughout the universe is well fed with abundant, healthy, nutritious food. You ask that the needs of all are taken care of. Your prayers for all who live in a multitude of societies on earth and throughout the universe are a hallmark trait of the Messiah.

Being a Messiah

Being a Messiah bears great responsibility. At times, you may feel a profound desire (an energy that touches all humanity) well up from the deepest part of your heart and soul that all suffering cease in the most appropriate and positive ways.

Your desire to serve and make a difference has become more important than your desire to be served and to neglect making a difference.

During any lifetime, including this one, you, the Messiah, care to see, know, experience, and share how to end human suffering and provide loving transformational guidance to anyone who asks for it.

The Miracles

The Miracles you perform are more private in nature; you are not going to part the Red Sea or the Pacific Ocean. As the Messiah, you quietly help spread the wisdom given unto you - that which flows through you - to others, helping to relieve suffering and guiding them back to inner peace.

CHAPTER 4

THE DOCTRINE

Behold, dear soul, your heart and allow the guidance of God to light the path in front of you.

There is never a need to know what is to be done at a different time. For you understand that the present-moment guidance is ever flowing every moment throughout every day, every week, and every year of your life. You trust in the will of God that encompasses providence for the entire human race.

Favor is brought upon you because your deeds are a reflection of what is to come in your life. The fear of judgment, or of not doing the right thing, is transformed into simple knowledge that each motive you have, each act you perform, and each intention you live out by the spiritual laws of the universe are never returned void. You and I, as Messiahs, will always reap tenfold measure of what we have sown.

The desire to please God has been transformed into the wisdom that you are a pleasure to God at all times, and it is not fear that rules your actions - it is love to do only that which you know in your heart is right.

The Religion

Ah, as many cultures, religions, and spiritual practices as there are, the Messiah knows that all of humanity is "being saved." Love is the savior. Integrity, compassion, loving action, and a pure heart are what create the Messiah's religion.

The Messiah doesn't hail from just one religion, even though he or she may have been born into a religion-specific culture. Just as the summer breeze blows with indiscriminate softness to ease the heat upon all faces, so, too, does the Messiah bestow divine love equally upon all people of all religions.

The serious and the playful, the hardworking and the pampered, those who buy and those who steal, as well as those who give and those who take - all are part of the inclusive divine plan in which every living soul is cared for.

The Messiah knows that particular foods, family traditions, and cultural and environmental teachings are respectively sacred to different people (including atheists) of the world. Atheists (exerting free will and choice not to believe in God at this moment of time) are as equally divine as either you or I.

With compassionate eyes, the Messiah looks upon those who would be judged by others who have not yet risen above judgment. The babe is born and learns what she or he is taught.

The Messiah understands that you are learning, as is the Messiah, with a gentle heart and a loving hand extended to all people. Most people (some call "sinners") work in fluctuating states of awareness, in varying combinations of positive and negative energy. The Messiah brings a heartfelt prayer of grace upon all people. The song of love in the Messiah's heart guides her or his views and perceptions. No longer is there judgment, only the sharing of wisdom and unconditional love that brings understanding.

But how does the Messiah share? He or she shares divine energy every sacred moment, alone or with others, most notably when opportunity arises.

The Messiah may write a book or send a note or a card, share a letter or a smile, or help a person who may be weakened by particular circumstances. She or he will always extend love and will never engage in bitter squalor.

The Messiah has too important a mission than to be involved in debate of society's views and discrepancies. While many are judging and debating, the Messiah is quietly helping, making a difference.

Self-Judgment

Within the inner sanctum of judgment lies self - judgment, of which the Messiah will have no part. Just as you learn from mistakes you made in life, so, too, has the Messiah learned from mistakes.

What God, All-That-Is, wants you to know is that the Messiah is not going to descend from a white cloud with angels and trumpets large enough for the entire human population to witness. Where would he land? Which part of earth? Which people would be deemed greater than others to receive him?

The answer is that the Messiah is not only among you, in every part of the world, but an intrinsic part of each of you. Human sufferings and trials of the heart have caused each of your hearts to open. Thus, love, understanding, and compassion for self transcends any self-judgment.

CHAPTER 5

☙

WHY THE MESSIAH?

For thousands of years, humanity has been waiting . . . for one person to descend from the sky . . . was it not "prophesized" that the day would come when heaven would reign and those on earth would be judged? Yes, but the Messiah knows that people on earth - including the "prophets" - are afflicted with debilitating self-judgment and, thus, create their own private hell on earth. The Messiah also knows that it is not God, the angels, or any other loving soul who judges humanity - it is Self. In this life and after this life, the awakened soul will look to see what he or she would have done better or differently.

The angels and God bring messages to humanity through humanity.

Do you think that if you saw a man fly from the sky and land on a nearby mountain top that you would bow your head, kneel down on your knees, and exalt his presence with a vow to follow only his words and instructions?

Know that through the fruits of heart-centered labor, from lifetime to lifetime, the Messiah's soul has grown in wisdom, like yours.

You inherently recognize truth when you see it, hear it, or read it.

The words of the Messiah will always be truth. It is such because God, All-That-Is, I-AM-THAT-I-AM, guides you and the Messiah (higher self) in what to say and do, along with when and how.

Holy and Humble

You are as holy as the Messiah is. You may already be humble, or you may still be growing into that awareness. You understand that holy does not mean boastful or to put on a show for planet earth's inhabitants to see. It is the opposite.

The holiness of the Messiah comes from the compassion and care radiating from his or her heart.

The Messiah will not debate or be involved in public displays of egocentric platitudes.

The Messiah is not "visible." Her or his work is done quietly and lovingly - as is yours much of the time.

The Song of the Messiah is instilled within each of us, all humanity, issued from the divine energy of All-That-Is.

The Song of the Messiah

Holy, holy is the Lord.

Holy, holy art thou.

You are protected each day.

You may rest at night.

You will know who I am when your heart feels love for all others.

Praise be to God. Praise be to all goodness.

Let the everlasting presence of the divine shine equally among all men and women and children.

Laughter eases the burden of the soul.

23

The song of the Messiah is the song of a smile.

Precious one, you are seen in clear and loving measure according to the growth of your soul.

Your soul reigns supreme with love.
Your eyes see with the look of love.
God has given you a special mission, filled with love.
Oh, I praise thee, my children of heaven and earth.
Oh, I love thee, who cannot do harm.
Oh, I beseech thee . . .
Who cares about the child's soul?
Who helps the older souls?
Who brings love, light, and hope to all souls?

Be still, my children, and listen, for as you feel divine love emanating from your soul, you will know that The Song of the Messiah is encoded in your hearts - love for yourself, for your neighbor, for your sister, for your brother, for all, even those whose hearts are in discord.

I present my life and share the secrets of God with you. God shares the same secrets with all. Oh, holy one, the secrets of the universe are profoundly simple. Yes, dear one, everything that carries the divine energy of creation carries the tone of love.

The angels bestow love and protection on you, your children, grandchildren, and great grandchildren. How becometh it is for you to open your heart to sing the Messiah's song.

When love is in thy heart - when it is only love in thy heart - you will be living the Messiah's song each moment for all the days of thy life.

CHAPTER 6

ॐ

THE REQUESTS OF THE MESSIAH

Being the Messiah carries responsibility that is nearly unfathomable. How can only one person "save" the entire human race generation after generation? Is someone actually going to live for the next few hundred years to see humanity evolve into its higher, finer, and more loving potential?

Can it be that there is more than just one Messiah?

How can just one individual save every person from every culture, representing every language spoken on earth? Where would the Messiah start? Who from which part of the world deserves to be saved first?

As almighty God has given you life, it is part of the divine plan for you to know how to re-create life as you envision heaven on earth to be.

The life force in you, and the Messiah, comes from God - the most powerful loving energy in the universe.

The Messiah bears witness to many lands of people who cry out to their Lord for help and salvation, for rest and ease, for food and warmth, for a cool breeze, and for the sweet quench of thirst.

Ah, the Messiah asks you to give your attention to the people who are dying and suffering, rather than to those who are boasting and showing off, without care for others in need.

The Messiah knows - and asks you to know - that there must be heart-centered awareness and compassion that replaces judgment. We cannot be for each other and against each other at the same time. Unified balance, with loving intention, creates the conditions for all to progress and thrive. As we grow, every person, including the Messiah, seeks help, wisdom, and divine guidance to be a living expression of his or her God-Self.

A Prayer of Deliverance

My dear Lord, how I beseech thee.

Show me how to rest.

Provide me with comfort but help all who are suffering before you help me.

May all who are suffering feel instant relief.

May all whose hearts feel broken and torn

receive the help they need so they can smile again.

May I be an instrument of All-That-Is

to help as many human beings as possible who are less fortunate than I.

Guide me, dear God.

Guide me, holy spirit.

Guide me, precious heavenly angels.

Guide me to bring deliverance to all, starting with myself.

CHAPTER 7

⚜

ALMIGHTY DEEDS

The Messiah will perform great acts of kindness and care that will be viewed as miracles. Because your heart is filled with the same love as the Messiah's, you will understand the role the Messiah plays and how you can bring miracles to those in need.

Compassion

The Messiah cares for all who have wronged. The Messiah shows compassion for all who are struggling. The Messiah brings a gentle smile, words of hope, and positive energy to everyone at every moment.

Peace

The Messiah will not, and cannot, ever create discord, trouble, war, violence, wrath, anger, or bring misery upon any person.

The Messiah brings transformation to humanity by being a part of humanity. Because the Messiah has seen the debilitating results of war - death from thirst, hunger, mortal wounds; overwhelming grief; and often, emotional and spiritual bankruptcy of those who survive - the Messiah can carry out only deeds of pure love and peace.

As such, you will never see the Messiah holding a gun. You will never see the Messiah be glad for another's sorrow. You will never see the Messiah bring harm to himself, herself, or another. The Messiah is a vehicle only for love.

Your Role

The Messiah will ask something of you. You will feel a calling from deep within your heart. You will know within every fiber of your being that the Messiah has actually spoken to you.

God reigns in heaven and on earth. The Messiah's role is to ensure that each person experiences deliverance from sorrow, that those who are healthy provide for those who are ill. The Messiah needs your help to uplift and help the entire human race transform into the gentle, loving greatness that every soul, which is part of the whole, already is on the inside. The Messiah asks you to help.

But how? How can I help the Messiah?

Ah, but the answer is simple. Always extend love to yourself, to those you come in contact with, to all beings - regardless of culture, race, creed, belief, or proximity.

Steer clear of anyone who is causing negative drama, harm, or feeding upon the misfortune of others.

The almighty God, of whom both you and the Messiah are equally part of, is sharing with you now what role the Messiah plays and how you fit into the plan to bring every being into a level of love, peace, joy, abundance, health, prosperity, and bliss.

Divine Instructions

Be not afraid of the chaos around you. Hold a picture in your mind of a peaceful earth. Hold a picture in your mind that shows all are fed. Hold a picture in your mind of nations that were once at war showering their neighbors with flowers instead of bullets.

Bring your mind into alignment with that which you would like to see unfold. Hold steadfast to your vision. Remain calm and certain amid outer chaos and discord. Remember to trust that you are always divinely guided and protected.

If you feel drawn to say or read a prayer . . .

A New Psalm of Salvation

Every moment the Lord keeps me safe.

As nations raise their weapons, I am protected from harm.

As stones, fire, flood, hurricanes, and earthquakes strike land,

I am divinely protected.

I, a child of God, fear not.

There is no wind that can blow me away.

There is no rain that can flood my abode.

There is no fire that can go out of control.

There is no storm or lightning that can ever harm me.

The one almighty God loves me and delivers me from danger.

I am protected by day and by night.

I am loved just as I am.

I am respected because of the might

that exists in the gentleness that I feel in my heart.

I, a child of God, remain still, as the Messiah asks me to remember who I am.

CHAPTER 8

❧

THE MESSIAH'S PLEDGE

This is a divine song blessed by God, given to humanity (you). It is a pledge that the Messiah is being reminded to remember:

I Shall Be as a Messiah

My dear God, when people plotted against me, when they sought to take everything away from me, when they sought to destroy my life, you guided me to safety.

As I cried, you heard me.

As I prayed, you answered me.

You showed me how to start anew after everything was taken from me, everything but the will to carry on and to create from my heart.

How fortunate I am to be your child.

The love you have shown me is incomparable.

Though I cried rivers of tears, you gently guided my heart to solace.

You replenished my soul.

You showed me how to smile again.

You gave me the answers that ended my pain.

There are no words that can thank you for all you have done for me, for the speedy action you brought upon those who tried to hurt me, as you stopped them.

You reminded me that I am never alone.

I give glory to the divine that exists within us all.

Please show me where I am needed.

Please help me to remember who I am.

Please give me the guidance to deliver myself, just as you have delivered me from sorrow and bondage, and the strength to help humanity deliver itself.

You freed me from the bondage of a broken heart.

You mended my soul.

You gave me the guidance to move forward as you lit the path ahead of me.

You showed me there is light even amidst the pitch darkness I experienced during the dark nights of soul.

When I wanted to die, you showed me why I should live.

When I wanted to take, you showed me why I should give.

When I wanted to brag, you showed me those who never boast.

When I wanted to give up, you showed me how to begin again.

For every day you have helped me, for every moment you sustained me, for every miracle you brought into my life, I shall be as a Messiah and join with the love of almighty God, Creator of heaven and earth.

Even the Messiah has seen the darkest of days.

I will show all how amidst the darkness there exists a brand new light, the light of divine love, eternal hope, a joy-filled life, unwavering care, perfect health, warmth and comfort - all of this and so much more are what the Messiah shows me.

Alas, I never knew I would be guided to remind the Messiah of who he is, she is, and I am.

CHAPTER 9

❧

REFLECTION

As you reflect upon this book, words, new psalms, and songs of the Messiah, take yourself a step closer to the mirror and look into your eyes. What do you see in your reflection? Ah, yes, you see a dear soul who has endured much, a soul who desires peace. You have glimpsed relief and comfort, and now you are being reminded that even a Messiah cannot force someone to decide to release his or her pain.

The decision of each soul is honored because each soul is endowed with free will, choice. Even a Messiah cannot convince you how lovable you are. Do you remember when someone complimented you, and it was difficult for you to believe the truth of the compliment? Did you know that you have seen the Messiah and the Messiah has seen you? But where? You ask. How? You wonder. You may claim, "I have not seen the Messiah."

Oh, yes, you have. When you look into your own eyes - the mirror of the soul - with divine stillness in your heart, you are being shown that you are a Messiah unto yourself.

CHAPTER 10

❧

HUMANITY'S SAVIOR

Has it dawned on you that you are here to bring salvation and goodness into your own life?

Do you think just one person who may have descended from a billowy cloud is the only person who can inspire you to honor the good (God) you have within you?

Do you think just one person can save you and your children, your friends and their children, and ongoing generations, as well as all those of previous generations?

What does "Salvation" Mean?

Salvation means that you have decided to create anew from where you are right now. With awareness and a loving heart, the divinity within is revealed, degree by degree, as you listen to your higher self and allow it to show you the next step to your own salvation.

Who is "the Savior"?

"Savior" means to be a savior unto yourself. The process by which the Almighty empowers one savior is the same process the Almighty - equally - empowers you. Again, approach the mirror and look into your eyes. There is a stillness present and a realization (shimmering through the fog of memory) that the light of the savior is the same inner light that is within you, yourself.

CHAPTER 11

୧

SAVE WHO FIRST?

Ah, you wonder, who shall the Messiah save first? Which person? From which race? From which part of the world? Which language will that person speak - Greek, Hebrew, Arabic, English, Spanish, Chinese? How can one Messiah favor another before favor is given unto you?

Do you think the man down the street should be saved first? What about the elderly woman? What about the little girl who is sick? Which child gets saved first - the child with cancer or the child with a bandage covering a deep wound? If a child burned in a fire was saved, the pain from the burns must be tended to first . . . wouldn't you agree?

So, too, the Messiah agrees that his or her role upon this earth is very much like your role upon this earth: the awakened conscience, the heart that steers clear of sorrow, the heart that cried a river of tears today and may cry again tomorrow.

Where is it written that there is only one Messiah? There has been a pervasive belief that one Messiah would arrive, save humanity, and then ascend up into the clouds, as if levitating above the earth. The Messiah does not need an airplane . . . or does he?

Do you, for a moment, believe that the Messiah can fly? Can you fly? Oh, my dear child, if I told you of your greatness, would you agree? If I told you of the power you hold within your mind, would you seek Me?

Dear soul, my precious child, just as life on earth grows and shifts season after season, century after century, so, too, does the Messiah grow from lifetime to lifetime.

If all are equal parts of God, how can there be just one Messiah?

Just as the ascended masters who carried humanity one step closer to heaven on earth - from Moses to Jesus, Mohammed to Buddha, from God to You - can it be that the responsibility to save your own life, via your own soul, is the reason you are here?

Do you want a better life? Do you desire to help make a difference for humanity? Yes, dear one, these and more are all signs of the Messiah.

Your soul can see forever . . . capturing eternal truth in one breath and eternity in one heartbeat. Try as the ego might, ego cannot see even tomorrow.

Can you envision a peaceful humanity? How do you believe humanity can become that way? Who do you think should be the leader of others? Or would you prefer that each person be a leader unto him- or herself? To govern self, save self, uplift self - which uplifts you, yourself - is that not better than giving up your divine inner sovereignty and, instead, following someone who, you've been told, should be your leader?

On the bare, humble ground the Messiah walks, but he forgot that he was the Messiah when he was born into this life. How can we remind him? Which person is she? The Messiah could never leave one soul behind - could you?

CHAPTER 12

NEGOTIATING THE DISTANCES

The Messiah travels great distances each day within his or her mind. He sees the tears of others and hopes they experience relief. Because her heart is always seeking to serve, seldom does she realize how far she has come. Can it be that you, as well, have forgotten how far you have come?

What capacity is it that a human being has that might be deemed the most important . . . a capacity more powerful than all others? Yes, that's right. It is the capacity to love. You knew the answer. How? How did you know the answer? Do you remember the time you learned that truth or were shown evidence of that truth by someone who lovingly helped you? Just like the deeds of those who have helped others - like the angel carrying a child out of harm's way - you, too, are here to lovingly help someone, to lovingly save someone . . . yourself. It is you that you are here to lovingly help, to lovingly save. Not another person, but solely you, yourself.

What would you think if a person came up to you, announced that he or she was the Messiah and proceeded to tell you what to do? Would you listen? Would you go along with that person? Would you invite that person into your home? Or would you tell that person to mind his or her own business and shut the door because you've been told the Messiah lived thousands of years ago, certainly not today in modern times . . . but wait . . . maybe it's possible . . . perhaps he does live today . . . perhaps she lives today. For how can there be only one Messiah responsible for the billions of people born throughout the countless ages of time?

The word of God has been brought to humanity, but too many religions have distorted or hidden the real truth. And so it is that much of humanity continues to search for an external savior, a savior outside of oneself, a savior who lived thousands of years ago, a savior who (it's been said) is supposed to "one day return."

CHAPTER 13

THE HOLY BIBLE

Why then, and how, was the Bible written with so much misinformation? Let us find out.

Truth is simple. So, too, are the explanations being given to those of you reading this right now.

It has been documented by religious scholars from all over the world that ancient gospels have been discovered . . . uncovered . . . that were excluded from the Bible, gospels that attested to the divine energy of God existing within each and every person on earth and that connection with the divine energy could be accessed from within by each individual.

Many people blame God for the woes of their human experience. Is this fair? Is it logical? Why do they blame God for that which is done of their own free will and choice?

Can it be that thousands of years ago "free will" among the masses was a scary concept for those who wrote the Bible and for those church authorities who wanted to establish control over the masses?

There is an assumption among many religions that the holy Bible was written and organized by "holy" people. Do you agree with that? So which one of those holy people is the savior? Any of them? Of the purportedly holy people who created the holy Bible, is one of them "the savior" of all humanity?

The Bible also encouraged the masses to believe that "one day" life would get better. And how would that happen? Why, of course, God would one day send a Messiah.

The pervasive belief that there is only one Messiah must be changed, for it is deceptive, and endeavors to steal the knowledge of the existing divinity from the hearts of people who love God, self, neighbor, friend, and relative.

Most people have forgotten that before coming into this life, they divinely understood they were to be Messiahs unto themselves. Is that too much to bear thinking about? Is that too difficult to understand? What about divine help? Can it be that the divine energy of God existing within each person is that which makes it natural to receive divine help from the divine Source of almighty God?

Yes, and what God would like to share with the most precious human race is that each soul who incarnated into this life did so with the understanding and agreement that full awakening of his or her own divine nature would be achieved. Full communion with God would become commonplace, an everyday occurrence.

Experiencing just a glimpse of heaven reveals a beauty and power so vast that you know you are seeing it through the eyes of your higher self.

A Reminder of Who You Are

Allow me please to remind you again of who you are.

You, as a Messiah, are responsible for yourself. Your life is what you create with it. Your soul remembers the people you have agreements with, and your soul even knows how to save you - once you remember how to access this inner wisdom given to you by God.

All people are given the same measure of divinity and equality. It is the people who choose to let their innate divine power shine through who realize one of the most powerful acts a person can do is to allow others to shine. How is that powerful? It displaces ego with the power of love working from the divine energy of "allowing." Divine love is inclusive and allows others, unlike ego that wants control and the spotlight.

Have you ever been transported by the beauty of a singer's voice . . . or transfixed by an elegant skater gliding effortlessly across the ice with arms and leg poised in air . . . by the grace of a swan or the inner balance of a sturdy, steady beam or the majesty of mountain, the grand sweep of plain, the fathomless power of the ocean's ebb and flow? It is humbling to bear witness to the endless spectrum of abilities, beauty, mystery, and infinite forms of life manifested from the same divine energy, the same heart of God that dwells equally not only in all beings, but in all matter.

The heart of God dwells equally in every house. Of course, some people may understand "house" to mean a physical structure such as a home, but spiritually, it is a metaphor for the physical body. Your house, or body that houses your soul, receives guidance and answers from the divine energy of your Higher Self or God.

People, especially those of different cultures, sometimes shun or distance themselves from others whose spiritual beliefs are obviously different (often indicated by clothing or speech) from their own. So . . . what would you do if you found yourself with someone whose views of God were obviously different than your own?

Why, you would lovingly accept that person and allow for their different beliefs because God is inclusive of all religions. If it were widely known and accepted that each person is a Messiah unto her- or himself, humanity would instinctively live more responsibly. People would hold themselves accountable for their actions.

Spiritual accountability is the hallmark of the Messiah. Why? Because it is the hallmark of love. To be spiritually accountable can only be rooted in love.

Any other energy negates the hallmarks of spiritual freedom. Just as an airplane is fueled to soar in the sky, the heart and soul of every person is fueled - encoded with the divine energy and knowledge of being one with the Creator - to soar in the higher realms of God. Since God is an indivisible part of every human being, no one can possibly "be left behind," as some religious teachings imply. How can anyone possibly be left behind when God's divine energy constantly lives within everyone? No matter who you are, where you go, or what you do, God's energy is a constant inner presence, lovingly and patiently waiting for you to become aware of It.

CHAPTER 14

PARTING OF THE SEA

Can you imagine how awestruck you would feel if you personally witnessed Moses parting the Red Sea? But wait a minute . . . perhaps you did witness that event. Perhaps you were there. How do you know you were not?

Prior to each lifetime, your soul, hungering and thirsting for the divine, wanted you to drink only the waters of divine wisdom and eat only that which would bear holy fruit so you could more easily know and feel yourself as divine as God . . . but getting to the point of actually "feeling yourself as divine as

God" is a process. So you made an agreement prior to entering each lifetime, the agreement being that each life would provide learning experiences until, eventually, there would be your final earthly life - the catalyst lifetime - when you would finally be ready and able to "save yourself" (becoming aware of the divine love and truth within yourself and allowing that divine energy to lead you in taking personal responsibility for yourself, for your own spirituality).

CHAPTER 15

HOLY INTERVENTION

Here now, my dear child, are the words of God given unto you, so that when the occasion arises, when you are looking for another to save you, you will be reminded to look only in the mirror.

Over thousands of lifetimes, humanity has pleaded and cried out to the Lord for help, hope, deliverance, and salvation. And after every lifetime, experiencing various degrees of growth, every soul returns to "the other side."

Yes, for thousands of years, humanity has been preparing for today. Throughout thousands of lifetimes - each one sacred - most people deemed themselves unworthy to be their own "saviors," so the same engrained feeling (lie) over countless lifetimes has been communicated to Self.

Each person in the human race bears the divine energy encoding of God on a cellular level. And every soul carries forth a mission: prior to each lifetime, each soul promises to remember that divine energy is encoded within him- or herself. But . . . after moving from the other side of the veil to this side - the next human life (this life) - most souls, not all, forget the promise they made.

Dear one, not only are you as spiritual as you are human, you are, in fact, more spiritual than human.

Your tears, trials, and lessons - all you've endured - have resulted in immeasurable growth that is culminating in this lifetime so you can finally move above the duality system of the earth school and permanently enter the new realm: the realm of heaven that exists within. Perhaps you felt, or were taught, that Heaven is a place that exists in the sky and above the earth. Dear One, the guidance given to you now is to know that you are the sole creator of the heaven you experience within. Heaven is not a destination, it is an experience, and one that you so dearly deserve to remain as you create and experience this as your new reality. And yet, for eons, you and the rest of the human race were taught and believed in the exclusion of one person being worthy of heaven, perhaps more so than another. And yet, this is a false belief, just as if you were to believe there is not a shining sun when you can see only clouds. Far too much of the human race has been taught to live with fear, least you would not be granted access through the gates of heaven, and in each lifetime your souls journey has glimpsed the true creator or heavenly experience, and the one who is responsible for creating your heavenly experience.

It is you! You are the one who decides from the calling you feel in the deepest part of your being to finally experience all love, all goodness, and all freedom of the Divine.

After each lifetime, returning to the other side, eager to view the life you lived and the growth you made, you were asked the question: "Why didn't you transcend self-doubt and take responsibility to save yourself?" And after each lifetime, your answer was the same: "I forgot."

The Journey within Eternity

You may have forgotten your promise during all the other lifetimes, but now you are being reminded of who you truly are so that you may continue your soul's growth in a higher, more gentle, loving realm.

This is the "salvation lifetime" that you have entered. These holy instructions given unto you are simple and the guidance as beautiful as eternal.

After all you have endured . . . it is time to make a choice. Do you want to return again to earth after this life for yet another opportunity to finally take full, loving responsibility for yourself, or do you want to accomplish it in this lifetime, so you can progress and continue to live and learn in the most loving system in the universe?

Ah, yes, it is time to invoke the sweet memory of soul's promise made not so long ago and remember that the only one who can save you is you!

Self-Deliverance

It is a holy time when a soul consciously realizes self-deliverance. The alternative is to remain a powerless victim of life's circumstances. Once you decide where you are going and how you wish to live, as certain as the sun will rise tomorrow morning, your role will be aided by many.

There is a divine orchestration of legions of angels who, as they whisk through space and so-called time, communicate with each other, helping you grow according to the measure of permission you have granted them. This period of time is one of the most important cycles in the development of the human race.

The Messiah's Religion

The only religion necessary to follow is love, combined with the Golden Rule, "Do unto others as you would have them do unto you."

Remember that God loves all people - not only those who worship among the various religions of the world, but those who don't have a particular religion, and those who, at this moment in time, may not believe in God at all.

Your Promise to Remember

How can you be aided to live and shine in a new life, free from the harsh conditions of those that exist on earth? By deciding you wish it to be so. By asking God, the divine within, to help you remember who you are and how to carry out your mission.

Remember that others are also Messiahs unto themselves, experiencing earthly life just as you are, but most have forgotten the truth of who they are. And as such, they may be searching the sky right now for a man riding a chariot in a billow of clouds heading straight for their neighborhoods.

Dear one, almighty God adores you and gives you the truth that will set you free - permanently.

Take your current concept of "Messiah" into your mind, and after you become aware of what it is you believe, ask God for insight and clarity into the spiritual truth of the matter. The realization that you, via soul, are a Messiah unto yourself is indeed the reality you promised you would remember - and asked to be reminded of - so that you can carry out your mission of spiritual sovereignty over yourself.

In the past, you have endured countless trials in a vast desert of illusion while thirsting for truth, but once you elevate yourself from within to experience your God Self, you will receive divine guidance and the sweet nectar of sacred knowledge. As you open your parched lips to drink, your thirst for spiritual truth will be forever quenched. All that is required is . . . that you ask for it.

CHAPTER 16

❧

LEADERSHIP AND POWER

A definitive quality exhibited from the depth of a Messiah's soul is leadership unto oneself. Let us now take the view that you came into this life to be reminded of how much you matter and how much of a difference you are here to make, starting with your own life.

"To lead" requires personal awareness of your own personal power. This is a deeply important aspect, or characteristic, of being a Messiah that is played out with a pure heart every moment of your life.

Your willingness to see beyond your current system of living - as you declare to yourself your desire to feel the most loving connection to God and state that you would like to know what, exactly, you are to do in this life - is that which will help the answers flow to you.

The reason you may have been looking for a specific person, outside yourself, to be your savior is because in ancient times when the Bible was written, it was said that a savior would one day come. The part that was omitted, the most important part, is that you will be a savior unto yourself. Every ascended leader led from the heart, and with humbleness has shared their recognition of the divine existing within all, equally. They did not place themselves above humanity they placed themselves as equally among humanity, eager to bestow their wisdom that every member of the human race is one with God and all others. Their recognition of the equal divinity among every man, woman and child made it lovingly heard and known that you are as holy as those to whom you worship and pray.

Cornerstones of Empowerment and Leadership

The guidance being shared with you now is that just as love, combined with an inner resolve to take your life and bloom in the most clear and certain ways, is a cornerstone of empowerment, so, too, is leading yourself (allowing yourself to be led) by the power of pure love.

Too many centuries of life on earth have been plagued with the false information that someone else is here, or will soon arrive, to save you.

In the most holy and pure way, each soul has been granted free will, choice. Yet, too many people look to others to guide them and walk them through their lives, the lifetime they (you) are currently in.

The power aspect of leadership must be conveyed as a firm resolve, such as the resolve to do only that which is right and to be honest and to never steal under any circumstances. These are a few of the basic traits of people who have recognized their ability to rise above fear and uncertainty in order to fully align with the higher truths they integrate into thoughts about themselves and the correlating beliefs and self-empowerment they uncover because of it.

I say "uncover" because most people, as they walk through life, are unable to realize they actually have authentic spiritual power (waiting to be harnessed) and leadership (waiting to be manifested) over themselves. They are still looking for another person to be their savior and have not realized that a true savior humbly and clearly carries out his or her life mission unencumbered by fear. And as that happens, doubts about self are washed away.

The delusional concepts you may have been taught regarding whom, exactly, to look to as your savior will no longer hamper your vision. It is now being asked of you to look in the mirror, with a sense of humility and clarity, so that as you gaze loving-ly into your eyes, you will see the spiritual essence of God.

True, Almighty Power

The power you have must never be used to hurt yourself or to control others. Being "of service" is an-other hallmark of true power.

It is the opposite of those who court power over others to attract followers. The Messiah, who can be likened to your higher self, will only help you discov-er and bring out the best you have within you. And it is now time for you to receive a simple list of char-acteristics, motives, and behaviors that a Messiah will exhibit once you are willing to embrace your authen-tic power in accordance with divine will.

The Characteristics

1. Sharing the desire to do only that which is right, all of the time.

2. The pure intentions and full willingness to be guided by God from within.

3. A Messiah helps others, yet never takes responsibility away from them. A Messiah is inwardly guided with wisdom and discernment and the power to carry out the higher guidance that he, she, and you have received and will always receive.

4. A Messiah is never conflicted. While being a beacon of light to inner freedom and security, the Messiah would never extol others to follow her or him. There cannot be egotistical traits interspersed with a few selfless days - just as there cannot be lies mixed with a few statements of truth. You must pick a path. Being a shining example of the divine, by following the guidance within, makes you a natural leader that others instinctively want to join. Those who try to get others to follow their lead by coercion or manipulation are being led by ego, their lower nature, instead of their higher nature.

This is one of the most important aspects of spiritual leadership: I lead only inasmuch as my actions lead by example. I never desire to control others; I desire only to serve with a pure heart.

5. Seeing yourself and all others through loving compassion and rising above judgment with balanced clarity are characteristics the Messiah has or is developing via personal growth in this lifetime. There is never a day when the opportunity to be an example of love does not exist.

6. Children are treated as the advanced souls that they are, and special attention is given to validate their unique expression of truth at all times. Children are dear to the Messiah.

7. The Messiah will never be involved in grandiose acts that inadvertently put people in danger. However, the Messiah may very well speak out for people, not caring if he or she has ruffled some feathers. Truth is the Messiah's only concern, combined with the love to carry it out.

Perhaps you remember, from books you may have read, how Nelson Mandela led his people purely from his heart, freed his people by persistently acknowledging truth, gave up his freedom for standing his ground, and finally changed the course of history for those who lived with apartheid.

He would have none of apartheid. And yet, he never used weapons to harm those who were the minority in power. Nelson Mandela's weapons were love and truth, along with the courage that sustained him through long years of hardship.

8. The Messiah quietly displays inner strength with the courage to carry out her or his mission, regardless of difficulties, based solely on guidance from the heart, according to divine will.

Innate abilities like inner strength and courage are timeless because they are unbreakable threads of the divine, which reside equally within each of us. Mandela was one who had exceptional insight at the time and found his divine center of inner strength within and steadfastly aligned with it.

9. Full alignment with divine will is never a chore to the Messiah. The honor of fully aligning your will with divine will is a sacred act that helps others by virtue of your example to share and demonstrate how the impossible is possible, after all.

CHAPTER 17

A TIMELESS BRIDGE

There is a timeless bridge anchored in the heart that connects you to the steadfast, narrow path of the inner Messiah as you retreat to the stillness within and let the divine guide you with the energy of wisdom and love. The Messiah could never tread the wider, negative path (crowded with reactionary views and actions - jealousy, fear, greed, manipulation, vanity, martyrdom, and hostility), just as a cat could never fly. It is not within the nature of either to do so.

The development of compassion will cause you to shine - every moment - regardless of what's going on externally. It is of utmost importance to give yourself permission to be and grow into your very best. Once you give yourself permission, directions are more easily seen on the narrow path. The timeless bridge to the narrow path of the inner Messiah is always surrounded by protection, just as you, yourself, are right now.

The bridge is crossed metaphorically every day, from one day to the next, aided by the steadfast traits and resolve that have become your foundation.

Divine Accomplishment

As the Messiah does great works, he or she will not take personal credit for those works but, instead, give credit to Source, God, Creator, All-That-Is, I-AM-THAT-I-AM. One of the most beautiful aspects of "being the Messiah" is being comfortable with humility.

Humbleness/humility is a hallmark that issues forth from the Messiah regarding any works he or she may do. If he sings a song, he gives God the credit for gifting him with musical ability. If she cooks for her children, she gives thanks to God for the ability to provide nourishment. And, of course, she never doubts that there will be more, for she knows that the Source of this universe is the same Source for all and is inexhaustible. The infinite Source will never run dry; it is eternal and keeps flowing to easily fill the needs of all who ask.

CHAPTER 18

⸎

A BLESSING FOR YOU FROM THE MESSIAH

As you have asked to be reminded of your true heritage, please take these words into your heart:

All the days of thy life you are called upon to bring humanity proof that the Divine brings forth a Messiah. And all the days of thy life you have looked to God for guidance, wondering who you are. I call on you to recognize who you are, so you will never again look to another fellow human traveler to be your savior.

My brother and sister, we are one race, one spiritual heritage, one Source, with divine love as the central core in each and every one of our hearts. Never toil searching for inspiration; you will receive the inspiration you need from your soul, your higher self, particularly when the physical body is at rest, asleep. The energy of your heart and soul are intricately connected to like energy on waves that span the ever-expanding universe, just as love spans eternity.

The saving grace you have been waiting for is already inside you. There is not another time when you will be more divine than now because the divine energy within you is always a constant. Being aware of the loving consciousness within you and then living within your higher consciousness so it becomes the foundation of your outer life is a process, a loving, living commitment that will lead you to your highest experience of self – your God-self.

Lift up your head. Lift up your heart. Let these words comfort you: Almighty God is within every breath you take. You will soon notice this as you experience more tranquil moments that assure you, by virtue of their clarity and peacefulness, how your heart can smile again.

Cultivating feelings of joy and gratitude brings forth the loving, causal energy to receive more of what you are grateful for.

You are divinely guided, loved, watched over and assisted by the angels who have always been and will always be with you. Remember to request assistance from the angels so you can receive immediate miracles in every area of your life.

Always keep your focus steadfast within each now moment awaiting the all-knowing higher guidance to awaken your consciousness and guide you gently from within.

When others create fear and drama you will immediately recognize it as such. Create a wave of loving compassion along with the hope that their consciousness awakens so they can experience true peace.

Remember your connection and spiritual heritage as God's energy eternally flows on waves of truth and love into your heart and mind. Allow this to be the guidance you rely on, your aid, support and source of comfort every moment of your life.

Your rise to the highest frequency of pure spiritual growth are equated with loving motives, transparency, humble responsible leadership by example, honesty, integrity, personal accountability, charity, hope, playfulness and gratitude. As you rise within to experience inner certainty and peace, remember to help others see the greatness they too, hold within by simply breathing.

Remember that you have a transparent protective shield of the highest energy frequency surrounding you that nothing of a lower energy can penetrate because it is as bright as the sun. Take comfort in knowing that as you rise within your awakening consciousness you will discern and allow only the purest energy to touch your life.

Honor every child and remember when you look into a child's eyes you are being reminded of the innocence, playfulness and love that is the hallmark of the Messiah.

You are that child. With every blessing in the universe you can playfully create more as you spread hope, peace, truth and ease into the hearts of many while you live the rest of your days with a divine smile in your heart, as you realize God resides there now and forevermore.

ABOUT THE AUTHOR

Barbara Rose, PhD is the bestselling author of eighteen books, a world renowned life transformation specialist and leading global spiritual teacher. She is a pioneering force in incorporating Higher Self Communication, the nondenominational study and integration of humanity's God Nature into modern personal growth and spiritual evolution. Dr. Rose is known for providing life changing answers, quick practical coaching and deep spiritual wisdom to people worldwide. She is the founder of International Institute of Higher Self Communication, and Global Humanitarian Religious Peace Treaty. Her renowned life transforming spiritual work is highly sought after internationally transforming the lives of millions across the globe. Dr. Rose's readers span over 180 countries. She works in cooperation with some of the greatest spiritual leaders of our time to uplift the spiritual consciousness of humanity.

Her official website is *borntoinspire.com*.

Made in the USA
Las Vegas, NV
27 March 2022

46388237R00059